SHOREDITCH

JANE BROCKET'S

CAPITAL
Tour

SHOREDITCH

yarnstorm
press

About the Brocket Pocket Guides This guide to Shoreditch is part of a series of *Grand Provincial Tour* and *Capital Tour Guides*, pocket-size publications which focus on the highlights and best aspects highlights of provincial towns and cities in Britain, and areas of London. They consider the pleasures and details that make up the spirit and contemporary cultural life of a place: art, galleries, buildings, markets, colour, patterns, cafes, baking, books, flowers, green spaces and places to swim. The emphasis is on having a good afternoon or day out, seeing and doing things that are accessible to all, don't cost a fortune, and don't require advance booking.

This guide also highlights the independent businesses which and help to make Shoreditch so refreshingly different to the rest of the capital, and champions the creative locals who contribute to its energy and evolution.

Book your ticket, and go. You will have a great time.

Jane Brocket created her popular *yarnstorm* blog in 2005 and has been blogging ever since, with frequent posts about London. She now writes the *yarnstorm press* blog (www.yarnstormpress.co.uk) and is the author of fifteen books on a variety of cultural and creative themes, many of which are illustrated with her photographs. She has spent thirty years both working in and visiting London, and is still as excited about the city as ever. She lives with her husband in Berkshire, close to a train station with a good service to the capital. They have three children who live and study in London.

Also available by the same author
The Grand Provincial Tour Guide to Preston

Forthcoming titles
The Grand Provincial Tour Guide to Coventry
The Grand Provincial Tour Guide to Oxford
The Grand Provincial Tour Guide to Norwich
The Capital Tour Guide to Soho and Fitzrovia

Contents

Introduction

Shoreditch is an immensely vibrant, characterful, historical part of London. Although it has come up in the world in recent years, it nevertheless continues to have the same diverse mix of smart and scruffy, rich and poor, historic and new, modern and old-fashioned that has characterised it for centuries, and it is this eclectic mix that makes it so gloriously relaxed and unstuffy, attractive and unpredictable.

Shoreditch has always been a place of varied and contrasting fortunes, and even now, with the recent arrival of cash, coffee drinkers, and independent, creative businesses, the make-over is not complete and there is still dilapidation that cannot be disguised. The current blend of cutting-edge style with this often down-at-heel local character means Shoreditch is a far cry from Kensington and Chelsea, and a stark contrast to the West End. Unlike those parts of London which seem to have fixed identities, Shoreditch has so far resisted definition, and continues to be in a state of energetic flux.

As a result, the visitor should bear in mind that small shops and businesses come and go all the time here, and therefore be prepared to take Shoreditch as he or she finds it on the day. No matter what, though, there is always plenty of offer for the curious visitor: pleasant urban wanderings, great Sundays, colourful street art, green-tiled pubs, Georgian churches, serious coffee, fine independent bookshops, galleries and cinemas, flowers, jam, cake, excellent bread, pots of tea, lots of bagels, vintage shops, markets, places to walk and cycle, sit and read, and beautifully made bags, socks, and boxer shorts. It may be best known at the moment as the home of hipsters, but the truth is that Shoreditch has such a friendly atmosphere and mixed bunch of locals and visitors, that no-one should feel out of place.

With such a rich mix of things to see and do, it's important to choose well and spend time wisely, and this is where this guide comes in. Instead of working its way through the usual listings and categories, it suggests a more creative and imaginative approach to visiting Shoreditch by considering common themes, patterns and details. So take your pick, mix, and have a good time.

COLUMBIA ROAD E.2.

Map

1. **OLD STREET** STATION, CAMDEN LOCK BOOKS, SHOREDITCH GRIND, SHOREDITCH TOWN HALL, ST LUKES, IRONMONGER ROW BATHS

2. **GREAT EASTERN STREET** HOXTON HOTEL

3. **PITFIELD STREET** ST JOHN'S, PITFIELD, BOOKART, PASSMORE EDWARDS LIBRARY

4. **LEONARD STREET** OZONE COFFEE, BOOK CLUB

5. **SHOREDITCH HIGH STREET** STATION, ACE/HOI POLLOI, ST LEONARD'S, MILK, TEA BUILDING, SHOREDITCH HOUSE (ON EBOR ST), COWLING & WILCOX

6. **KINGSLAND ROAD** FLOWERS GALLERY, GEFFRYE MUSEUM, FABRIQUE, HOXTON STATION

7. **ARNOLD CIRCUS** ROCHELLE CANTEEN, BOUNDARY ESTATE

8. **CALVERT AVENUE** LEILA'S, ALLY CAPELLINO, PAPER AND CUP, SYD'S COFFEE STALL, LUNA AND CURIOUS

9. **BOUNDARY STREET** ALBION/BOUNDARY, DISHOOM

10. **REDCHURCH STREET** ALLPRESS, BURRO E SALVIA, AUBIN CINEMA, AESOP, TRACEY NEULS, FRANZE & EVANS, LABOUR & WAIT, OWL & PUSSYCAT, SUNSPEL, MURDOCK

11. **BETHNAL GREEN ROAD** E PELLICI, RICH MIX, BRICK LANE BIKE, BOX PARK

12. **HOLYWELL LANE** VILLAGE UNDERGROUND

13. **RIVINGTON STREET** RIVINGTON PLACE, ARTWORDS, MATERIAL, TRAMSHED, TOWN HALL EXTENSION

14. **CITY ROAD** BUNHILL FIELDS, WESLEY'S CHAPEL

15. **BRICK LANE** BEIGEL BAKE, BRICK LANE COFFEE, TRUMAN BREWERY, BRICK LANE BOOKSHOP, CHESHIRE STREET SHOP, QUAKER COURT (CRESCENT TRADING)

16. **PAUL STREET** PRINCESS OF SHOREDITCH

17. **COLUMBIA ROAD** FLOWER MARKET, ANGELA FLANDERS, SUCK & CHEW, ROYAL OAK, LILY VANILLI, VINTAGE HEAVEN/CAKEHOLE, KEEPING CHOOSING

ST LUKES & IRONMONGER ROW BATHS

OLD ST A5201

A501

GEFFRYE MUSEUM Hoxton Station

GEFFRYE ST

DUNLOE ST

HOXTON ST

CREMER ST

HACKNEY RD

KINGSLAND RD A10

HACKNEY RD A1208

COLUMBIA ROAD ⓱

❸

PITFIELD ST

HOXTON ST

OLD ST

VIRGINIA RD

CALVERT AV

SWANFIELD ST

❻

OLD ST ❶

❶⃝ ⓭

RIVINGTON ST

RIVINGTON ST

CURTAIN RD

ARNOLD CIRCUS ❼

BOUNDARY ST

CAMLET ST

CLUB ROW

BRICK LN

PAUL ST

❺

❾

❹

A1202

GREAT EASTERN ST

LEONARD ST

❷

SHOREDITCH HIGH ST

REDCHURCH ST

❿

BETHNAL GREEN RD

❶❶

BRICK LN

LUKE ST

HOLYWELL LN

EBOR ST

CHANCE ST

A1209

SCRUTTON ST

⓬

SCLATER ST

RTH ST ⓰

CURTAIN RD

Shoreditch High St Station

PAUL ST

HOLYWELL ROW

CURTAIN RD

⓯

BRICK LN

WORSHIP ST

BISHOPSGATE A10

COMMERCIAL ST A1202

Free art
and galleries

Shoreditch is packed with visual interest. The people, flowers, window displays, little gardens, cafés, tiles, posters, lettering, and buildings all create a series of ever-evolving, wonderfully interesting *tableaux vivants*. But there is also a great mix of ultra-cool contemporary art, exuberant street art, and quiet domestic art which can all be seen for free.

Shoreditch street art Shoreditch provides a huge canvas for big pieces of bold, colourful street art which pops up on many buildings, walls, shutters, doors, railway arches and even meter boxes; in doing so, it has created what is effectively London's biggest public art gallery. It really does pop up, then it disappears, or is painted over; the art is temporary and the ephemerality is part of the appeal, and it means you have to enjoy it while you can as you may find something very different in its place on your next visit.

These days, this is definitely art rather than graffiti, and it's mostly above-board and sanctioned. Street Art London works with well-known street artists here in Shoreditch, many of whom prefer to use a pseudonym and/or remain anonymous, and big names of this creative world are often invited to create new pieces of work in prominent places (the huge VU wall on Great Eastern Street is one of the most prestigious locations). It forms a brilliant, colourful, free gallery of art which has vibrancy, energy, inventiveness, wit and sometimes, strangeness, aggression, and darkness. Some is simple (the brilliant stick figures by Stik) and some is complex (the clever ribbon/bandage images by Otto Schade). There are huge faces with grimaces and gritted teeth by Malarky; Dscreet's big-eyed, sharp-clawed owls; enormous words in fairground-style lettering by Eine. If you look carefully you'll also find all sorts of smaller stencilled figures, cartoons, animals, and creatures in the oddest places.

A leisurely street art wander is a great way to spend an hour or so outside; pick up a coffee as you go, pass a graffiti tour or two - or join one. If you are doing a DIY tour, the best places are Redchurch Street and the small streets off it (Ebor Street, Chance Street, Whitby Street, Camlet Street, Club Row, Turville Street, Swanfield Street), Sclater Street, Brick Lane, Cheshire Street, and the Village Underground Wall on Great Eastern Street.

Guided tours Street Art London runs tours every Tuesday (two hours), and Saturday and Sunday (four hours) which start at Old Street station. Email in advance, details on the website. (www.streetartlondon.co.uk)

Shoreditch Street Art Tours leads morning and afternoon tours which last three/three and half hours. Check the schedule on the website to see when they are on (usually every weekend and various weekdays). (www.shoreditcharttours.co.uk)

Rivington Place In a strikingly modern, very geometric building designed by architect David Adjaye in 2007, Rivington Place is home to INIVA (Institute of International Visual Arts), the Stuart Hall Library, and Autograph ABP which organises the artistic programme here. Its aim is to encourage 'art, debate, diversity' and to 'reflect the cultural diversity of contemporary society' and there is a lot happening here (events are mostly free). The galleries are rather bare and austere, and the exhibitions tend towards the abstract and conceptual, but it's all very thought-provoking. The busy Shutterbug Café, which is good for coffee and all-day breakfast during the day, turns into a noisy 'cocktail and crêpes' venue on evenings later in the week with music and yard parties.

i OPEN DURING EXHIBITIONS TUES, WEDS, FRI 11-6, THURS 11-9,
SAT 12-6, CLOSED SUN-MON
SHUTTERBUG OPEN MON-WEDS 9-6, THURS 9-MIDNIGHT,
FRI 9-1AM, SAT 12-1AM, CLOSED SUN

➤ RIVINGTON PLACE TEL 0207 749 1240

@ WWW.RIVINGTONPLACE.ORG WWW.SHUTTERBUG-LONDON.COM

Flowers Gallery A well-known gallery with serious modern art and photography displayed in a huge, plain, white space which was once used as a laundry and fur storage facility. The gallery was opened in the 1980s by the far-sighted Angela Flowers and although it may appear exclusive and slightly intimidating from the outside, in fact visitors are welcome to wander round and look at whatever is on show. The gallery also sells a selection of specialised art books.

i OPEN TUES-SAT 10-6

➤ 82 KINGSLAND ROAD TEL 020 7920 7777

@ WWW.FLOWERSGALLERY.COM

The Geffrye Museum This is unmissable, a beauty of a gallery devoted to the history of the home, and is worth visiting just for the wonderful building and garden, even if you are not interested in how domestic living rooms have evolved over the last four hundred years. The Geffrye is located in beautiful, plain, and graceful former almshouses which were built in 1714 and were used as such until 1912, when the London County Council converted them into a museum related to the local furniture industry. The museum later developed the series of eleven period rooms which show the development of English, middle-class domestic taste, fashion and style. It's fascinating to see both the structure of the original building with its chapel, the meticulous recreation of exhibition rooms, and the excellent collection of paintings. Outside there is a herb garden and various period gardens which are always full of flowers and colour (see page 55). It's free go inside although there is a charge for temporary exhibitions. The gallery also has a spacious, pleasant café, and a good bookshop with a very wide range of titles on relevant subjects such as architecture, social history and the home. In addition, one of the almshouses has recently been restored to how it looked in 1780 and is occasionally open to visitors (check the website for details).

i OPEN TUES-SUN 10-5, CLOSED MON UNLESS BANK HOLIDAY, 24-26 DEC, 1 JAN

▶ 136 KINGSLAND ROAD TEL 020 7739 9893

@ WWW.GEFFRYE-MUSEUM.ORG.UK

THIS PAGE *Fresh veg at Albion*
OPPOSITE *Bunhill Fields*

Fresh bagels
and sticky buns

Several businesses in this part of London are fine, modern practitioners of traditional baking and have been instrumental in the recent resurgence of interest in excellent cakes, buns, breads and pastries which put taste and texture ahead of looks and colour. The places below are not the only places to go to for good baking (see also Lily Vanilli, Albion and Leila's) but they are in this section because they are associated with one particular speciality which *'vaut le détour'* ('is worth the detour') as they say in Michelin Guides.

Bagels at Beigel Bake Beigel Bake is the place to go if you are a night owl, early bird, or just suddenly ravenously hungry at 3am. It is open 24 hours, all week, and produces seven thousand authentic, chewy, dense bagels a day. On the wall there is a marvellous price chart based on buying in multiples of half dozens and dozens which is a great way to be reminded of your six and twelve times tables: 144 bagels work out ridiculously cheap if you are planning a bagel party. Buy a bag of plain bagels or go for a traditional filling such as hot salt beef or smoked salmon and cream cheese. Plan your order as you wait in the queue as there's not much patience if you hesitate at the till, and eat your bagels soon after purchasing: like all good, real bagels, they don't keep for long.

 OPEN 24 HOURS

 159 BRICK LANE   TEL 020 7729 0616

BEIGELS

½	Dz	£ 1.50		8	Dz	£24.00
1	Dz	£ 3.00		8½	Dz	£25.50
1½	Dz	£ 4.50		9	Dz	£27.00
2	Dz	£ 6.00		9½	Dz	£28.50
2½	Dz	£ 7.50		10	Dz	£30.00
3	Dz	£ 9.00		10½	Dz	£31.50
3½	Dz	£10.50		11	Dz	£33.00
4	Dz	£12.00		11½	Dz	£34.50
4½	Dz	£13.50		12	Dz	£36.00
5	Dz	£15.00		12½	Dz	£37.50
5½	Dz	£16.50		13	Dz	£39.00
6	Dz	£18.00		13½	Dz	£40.50
6½	Dz	£19.50		14	Dz	£42.00
7	Dz	£21.00		14½	Dz	£43.50
7½	Dz	£22.50		15	Dz	£45.00

Swedish buns at Fabrique The location of London's best Swedish buns on a narrow street behind the Geffrye Museum in one of the arches of the new Hoxton Overground station doesn't make them easy to find, but once you have sampled them, you will remember how to get back for more. They are made by Fabrique, a Stockholm-based business, which sticks to doing a few things very well. It's mostly a bakery with a little sales and seating area (there are more seats outside) and is very plain and simple, with huge sacks of flour and flour-dusted bakers around the place, old-fashioned secretarial swivel-chairs and dark, strong, Swedish coffee in enamel mugs. The breads are big and wholesome (sourdough, rye, walnut and so on), the croissants and pains au chocolat are delicious, but it is the buns that make the journey worthwhile. Choose between cinnamon and cardamom, get an Americano with hot milk on the side, and enjoy a deliciously spicy, sweet, buttery, chewy and exceptionally sticky experience.

i OPEN TUES-FRI 8-6, SAT-SUN 10-6, CLOSED MON

❱ ARCH 285, GEFFRYE STREET TEL 020 7033 0268

@ WWW.FABRIQUE.CO.UK

Eccles cakes at St John Bread and Wine Justin Gellatly has moved on to Bread Ahead at Borough Market, but his amazing Eccles cakes live on at St John Bread and Wine in Spitalfields. These are not Eccles cakes as you may know them, but super-turbo-charged versions with incredibly flaky, buttery pastry and the densest, darkest, most curranty filling you are ever likely to encounter. Eat in with a piece of Lancashire cheese and a glass of Madeira, or take home a few in a bag. The St John loaves of bread, especially the sourdough, are also fantastic.

i OPEN FOR BREAKFAST 9-11, LUNCH MON-FRI 12-3, SUN 12-4, SUPPER 6-11, SUN 6-11

⟫ 94-96 COMMERCIAL STREET TEL 020 7251 0848

@ WWW.STJOHNGROUP.UK.COM

Chelsea buns at Rochelle Canteen Press the buzzer, enter the garden, take a seat and enjoy one of the best Chelsea buns you'll find anywhere, even Chelsea. Rochelle Canteen is in a converted school bike shed with tables and chairs that spill out into a courtyard area where, in summer, tubs and sinks and pots filled with tomatoes, geraniums, vines and cosmos form the backdrop. Breakfast is an informal but civilised affair, served from 9 to 11.30 with a super-simple menu (granola, toast, eggs, juice, tea, coffee). The Chelsea buns, made by head chef Anna Tobias, are the ultimate elevenses fare: soft, doughy, delicately spiced spirals with more and more sweet, sticky fruit the closer you get to the centre. Lovely. See page 39 for details.

Coffee fixes

It's a bit of an understatement to say that coffee culture is very much a part of modern Shoreditch. Every street seems to have a little café with a tiny, missable sign and stripped-back dark wood/blackboard/white wall décor. But even if you are a little allergic to the fashionable pursuit of the ultimate coffee, there is no getting away from the fact that these independent cafés are an enormously welcome alternative to the big coffee chains. They have interesting interiors, and are relaxed places to meet, chat, work, rest, and read.

Ozone Coffee Roasters Although this is owned by a New Zealand company, it's like stepping into modern Brooklyn, with exposed bricks, metal staircases, huge windows, painted signs and scuffed woodwork. This brilliant interior looks as though it's still just as Ozone found it, but is in fact very carefully designed and put together from scratch. Downstairs is the roastery, and upstairs are fresh coffee aromas, bustle and noise. Coffee is taken seriously, but if that's not your thing, they also do good hot chocolate and milkshakes. To eat, there are freshly baked cakes, pastries and sweet treats, a great number of ways with eggs on the all-day menu, and an all-day brunch at the weekend.

i OPEN MON-FRI 7.30-5, SAT-SUN 9-4 (KITCHEN CLOSES AT 3 WEEKDAYS, 3.30 WEEKENDS)

)) 11 LEONARD STREET TEL 020 7490 1039

@ WWW.OZONECOFFEE.CO.UK

Allpress In a plain and functional building is the simple and good Allpress Roastery and Café where you can watch beans being roasted as you enjoy an excellent flat white/espresso/latte/mocha, read the newspapers provided, eat a sandwich with an adventurous filling, enjoy a scone or a piece of cake, chat to friends, have a break from work, or just be. Allpress, with its neat, 60s style zippy logo, is a New Zealand company which been roasting coffee since 1986, and its tried-and-tested formula of good tasting coffee and fairly priced food clearly works well, as this place almost bursts at the seams at busy times. The café is light and simply done out with utilitarian chairs and tables (the effect is to make it look as though it's done on a modest shoestring) and there are benches outside in fine weather. There's a very relaxed atmosphere and a mix of coffee drinkers and, as well as the great coffee, beans and logo, Allpress can also boast an excellent location on Redchurch Street, close to all the good things in Shoreditch.

i OPEN MON-FRI 8-5, SAT-SUN 9-5

❯ 58 REDCHURCH STREET TEL 020 7749 1780

@ WWW.UK.ALLPRESSESPRESSO.COM

Fix 126 An archetypal Shoreditch coffee place with the *de rigueur* brown/black/white palette, natural textures, exposed brick, chipboard tables, school chairs, and simple light fittings. It uses its own blend which is true to the 'sweet, smooth, strong' tag, and the casual room is a good place to have an unhurried coffee with a fresh pastry or piece of cake and a chat. Alternatively, read your way through some of the printed material on offer which includes the *East End Review*, an excellent, free, local newspaper-style arts publication with good articles and reviews.

i OPEN MON-FRI 7-7, SAT-SUN 8-7

▶ 126 CURTAIN ROAD (ALSO AT 161 WHITECROSS STREET) TEL 020 7739 7829

@ WWW.FIX-COFFEE.CO.UK

Shoreditch Grind If you leave Old Street tube station by exit 8 you emerge by Shoreditch Grind, the high spot on a dismal roundabout (now branded 'Silicon Roundabout' because of the number of web-based start-ups that have proliferated here). It looks like a very small circular cinema, but instead of advertising the latest Cary Grant or Elizabeth Taylor film, the old-fashioned cinema lettering spells out a message above the door, usually something witty and topical. It's a café by day and a bar by night, and is always busy with a mix of locals and city suits. Although it may at first glance appear a little too self-consciously cool, it's actually a great place for a coffee and a Portuguese custard tart or croissant. The stripped-back interior is full of light due to the huge glass walls which get nicely steamed up in cold weather in the way that cafés used to, the brick walls are whitewashed, and the chairs are vintage, school style. Own-blend coffee is served with the usual Shoreditch attention to detail and reverence (which means it can take a while) and the menu covers simple breakfast bites, and salads, sandwiches and soups at lunchtime. Shoreditch Grind is a good location to watch the world go by from a perch by the window, and for post-5pm cocktails, wine and beer.

i OPEN MON-THURS 7-11, FRI 7-1AM, SAT 8-1AM, SUN 9-7

» 213 OLD STREET TEL 020 749 7490

@ WWW.SHOREDITCHGRIND.COM

Leila's You can buy excellent Coleman coffee (ground or beans – I recommend the Espresso blend) from Leila's shop or go into the café for a cup of Coleman coffee and a fine brownie. See page 37 and page 83 for more on Leila's.

CASH ONLY

ALLPRESS
ESPRESSO
"At Allpress it is all about flavour... starting
in Costa Rica and finishing in your cup. This
PRESS
ESSO

Breakfast,
lunch, dinner

BREAKFAST Franzè and Evans (see page 39), Rochelle Canteen (see page 39) and Hoi Polloi in the Ace Hotel (page 112), are also high on the list of good locations for breakfast in Shoreditch.

Albion A modern variation on the classic greasy spoon caff - without the grease. Albion is part of the Conran empire and it shows in the attention to detail, the relaxed atmosphere and the beautifully plain and simple room with traditional café references. It's light and airy with pretty flowers dotted about, a high ceiling, huge windows, and doors that are open to the street in fine weather. There are piles of newspapers, nice groupings of condiments, golden syrup tins to hold cutlery, sturdy tea pots, a well-stocked cake table, a kitchen and bakery on show, a great little shop for bread and baked goods, and nice jams and teas. Albion does a good choice of plain, hearty breakfast options in a relaxed and unhurried environment; it is nearly always busy and chatty and is equally good for elevenses, a meal from the all-day menu with many traditional British dishes, or simply a glass of wine. The kitchen brings out more good, baked treats in the afternoon between 3.30pm and 5.30pm.

i OPEN 8 TILL LATE DAILY, KITCHEN CLOSES AT 11PM,
BREAKFAST MON-FRI 8-MIDDAY, SAT-SUN 8-12.30

❱ 2-4 BOUNDARY STREET

@ WWW.ALBIONCAFF.CO.UK

Leila's Leila McAlister is the real-life Leila behind this café and grocery on Calvert Avenue which, with Boundary Street, bears a close resemblance to New York's Meatpacking District and has the same sort of interesting independent businesses in what were previously neglected and run-down buildings. Leila's early twentieth-century premises, though, have already had a previous incarnation as a grocer's shop, and comprise two handsome, double-fronted old shops. The café has more than a touch of the bohemian, and is known for its amazingly good fried egg breakfasts and high quality Coleman coffees, but the same devotion to good ingredients cooked with confidence continues throughout the day with salads and soups, and Leila's renowned brownies. Brunch at the weekend is worth getting up for early and combines well with a trip to Columbia Road (page 74). More about Leila's shop on page 83.

ⓘ OPEN WEDS-SUN 10-6, SUN 10-5, CLOSED MON-TUES

❱❱ 15-17 CALVERT AVENUE TEL 020 7729 9789

@ FACEBOOK PAGE AND TWITTER

Pitfield Pitfield is useful to know about if you find yourself around Old Street or are en route to St John's Church (page 53) and need somewhere pleasant and pretty for a simple breakfast. It opens early and has a short menu based around toast and croissants, tea, coffee and juice, served in the light and pleasant café area of an 'eclectic emporium' which also has a homewares and furniture shop and a gallery.

ⓘ OPEN DAILY 7-7, SHOP OPEN 11-7

❱❱ 31-35 PITFIELD STREET TEL 020 7490 6852

@ WWW.PITFIELDLONDON.COM

Dishoom Dishoom revives the concept of the old Irani cafes in Bombay in which different communities could come to eat, drink, meet, read, talk and socialise, and the Shoreditch version aims to capture the eccentricity and faded elegance of a 1930s café. There are many cultural crossovers in the food and drink, which make for breakfast dishes such as fried eggs on chilli cheese toast, sausages in naans, masala beans, and Bombay omelettes. Venture beyond tea and coffee with lassi and chai, sit on the verandah, and read a newspaper with your breakfast.

i BREAKFAST IS SERVED 8-11.30 MON-FRI AND 9-12 SAT-SUN.

OPEN MON-WEDS 8AM-11PM, THURS-FRI 8AM-MIDNIGHT,

SAT 9-MIDNIGHT, SUN 9AM-11PM

⟩⟩ 7 BOUNDARY STREET TEL 020 7420 9324

@ WWW.DISHOOM.COM

E Pellicci If you are up and about early and fancy a classic, no frills, plate-filling fry-up from 7am onwards, make your way here to one of London's most wonderful café interiors. See page 108 for more details.

LUNCH Leila's (page 37), Albion (page 36), Hoi Polloi (page 112), Pizza East (see page 42), and St John Bread and Wine (page 27) are also recommended for lunch.

Rochelle Canteen If there is one place that sums up the creative, thoughtful, civilised approach to life, the universe and food in Shoreditch, it is Rochelle Canteen. Melanie Arnold and Margot Henderson adopt an undoubtedly purist approach to simple preparation of extremely good, seasonal ingredients with a short menu in the ultra-plain room of a converted bike shed of the former nineteenth-century Rochelle school. It's a daytime/weekday-only restaurant, an open secret which is available to all as long as you can find the right door and buzzer on Arnold Circus. In good weather, the glass doors are drawn back and tables are put out in the courtyard garden, but the place buzzes with contented customers and food satisfaction at all times of the year.

i OPEN MON-FRI 9-4.30 (BREAKFAST 9-11.20, LUNCH 12-3, TEA 3-4.30)

➤ ARNOLD CIRCUS TEL 202 7729 5677

@ WWW.ARNOLDANDHENDERSON.COM

Franzè and Evans There is such a good choice of cool, hip places to eat and drink in Shoreditch, it's possible to overlook a café-deli which is fresh, bright, clean, relaxed and friendly but not falling over itself to be 'on trend'. Franzè and Evans has a great location near Brick Lane with tables on the pavement on Redchurch Street, making it a lovely place to sit in the sun with a big, tasty salad or plate of 'Tuscan eggs'. Retreat inside on colder, wetter days for a lunchtime lasagne or burger. It's not just good for lunch, though, as breakfast is served until 11, and there is a marvellous selection of cakes and baked good available all day long.

i OPEN MON-WEDS 8AM-7.30PM, THURS-FRI 8AM-11PM, SAT 9AM-11, SUN 9.30AM-7PM

➤ 101 REDCHURCH STREET TEL 020 7033 1910

@ WWW.FRANZEEVANS.COM

DINNER A menu of options:

Relaxed, noisy pizza option: book ahead for good, wood-fired pizzas in **Pizza East** in the Tea Building (see page 42).

Smart, plush option: the **Boundary** (see page 78).

Arty, meaty, poultry option: **Tramshed** (see page 46).

Noisy, casual, vast menu option: **Hoi Polloi** (see page 112).

Smart gastro-pub option: **The Princess of Shoreditch** (see page 77).

Hot dog and beer option: **The Owl and the Pussycat** (see page 78).

Traditional boozer option: **The Royal Oak**, Columbia Road (see page 79).

Nice pub with decent food option: **The Fox**, 28-30 Paul Street.

OPPOSITE *Franzè & Evans, Redchurch Street*

F & E

BRUNCH   BAKERY

SALADS   PANINI

COFFEE   BIBITE

Building history

Even if you know nothing about the history of Shoreditch, you can read it very clearly in its buildings. Until recently, these have been mostly low-rise - only the church steeples reached high above ground level - and a mix of warehouses, shops, dwellings and small-scale industrial buildings ranging from the smart to the almost derelict. Now, though, the sky-line is changing with immense, shiny new blocks looming over the old, small-scale Shoreditch; this is an area that is changing rapidly, and now is the time to go, before it loses its very human scale and interest, and while you can still absorb its history as you walk around.

TEA, 56 Shoreditch High Street This is the huge building next to the bridge and railway line with the big TEA sign on top. It was built in several phases between 1890 and 1930, and is called the Tea Build-ing because it was built for the Lipton family who made Lipton's teas so famous. It fills a whole block, Manhattan style, and the main High Street façade is classic 1930s with fine brickwork, windows and detail-ing. The building has been simply and plainly refurbished for genuinely 'mixed use' and is now home to various creative businesses, Shoreditch House club and hotel, and Pizza East. Inside, the original structure and bones of the place have been retained, and it's still clear and easy to see that this was originally a brilliant piece of twentieth-century warehouse architecture.

Passmore Edwards Free Library The Passmore Edwards Free Library (now apartments and the Courtyard Theatre) on Pitfield Street was opened in 1897, and is worth looking at to understand just how much visual importance and architectural interest can be attached to a library. It is unmissable: exuberantly bright red, with late Victorian Gothic flourishes and two wonderful book-reading female figures over the Pitfield Street entrance. Like many libraries in this part of London, it was funded by the Cornish philanthropist John Passmore Edwards. He was responsible for the creation of the distinctive, once-important libraries that still bear his name, as well as the South London Gallery in Camberwell and Whitechapel Gallery, both of which have fabulously rich Art Nouveau/Arts and Crafts exteriors which prefigure Edwardian exuberance and ornamentation. More Passmore Edwards libraries include Plashet, Bow, Plaistow, Stratford, Limehouse and Whitechapel (nice façade above Aldgate East Station). Some are still in good condition and proclaim the joys and value of reading and books even if they are no longer libraries, while others are looking very neglected. It is a shame that such a rich architectural and literary legacy is going to waste.

'More Light, More Power' In the late nineteenth/early twentieth century, Shoreditch had a very progressive local government which prided itself on its provision of electricity to the borough, despite it not being a prosperous part of the capital. Several buildings still attest to the importance of electricity here, and if you look carefully at the façade of the Town Hall on Old Street, and on the front of its 1930s 'Red Brick Annexe' (81 Rivington Street, now offices) you can see the Soviet-esque motto 'More Power, More Light'. The theme is extended to the tower above the entrance of the Town Hall which has a female statue of Progress holding a burning torch – and a battle-axe.

THIS PAGE *St Luke's, Old Street*
OPPOSITE *Shoreditch Town Hall*

PROGRESS

The Vestry of St Leonard Shoreditch Electric Light Station (1897) on Coronet Street in Hoxton is now home to the National Centre for Circus Arts (see page 102) where the vast generating and combustion chambers of the power station are ideal for flying about on trapezes and juggling high balls. It was also known as the Shoreditch Vestry Generating Station and Dust Destructor, as this is where local rubbish was brought to be burned to provide steam for the electric generator and heat for the public baths. Its motto, still there in terracotta letters above the entrance, was '*e pulvere lux et vis*' or 'out of dust, light and power', which makes one think of the dust heaps in Dickens' *Our Mutual Friend*.

At 32 Rivington Street is the cavernous, listed Tramshed, now occupied by a Mark Hix restaurant with the Cock and Bull Gallery underneath (www.chickenandsteak.co.uk). Its architect was the eminent E Vincent Harris who designed it in 1905 as an electricity generating sub-station for trams, and it's now a fine, post-industrial, white-tiled place to eat good chicken and steak as you consider the huge Damien Hirst vitrine containing a pickled cow with a chicken on its back which rises above the room.

Boundary Estate Shoreditch's notorious Old Nichol slum was pulled down and replaced in 1890s by the Boundary Estate (opened 1900) which was built to provide some of the first council housing in the world. The blocks of flats, which are listed, have a great deal of good striped and/or glazed Victorian brickwork and detailing. They radiate out from Arnold Circus whose mound was made with the rubble of the 'rookery' and is now covered by mature plants and trees and topped with a bandstand. The estate still has all the original housing and school buildings (the Rochelle School is now an arts centre, with Rochelle Can-

ROCHELLE
STREET
SCHOOL
1899

teen in the old bike shed) and each block is named after a clean, green town or spot along the Thames (which must have something of an irony when they were built). The whole estate is still very much a thriving Shoreditch community.

Village Underground The Village Undergound is a cultural centre on Holywell Lane and the trains which are apparently perched precariously above it on the Great Eastern Street side are in fact carriages which have been converted to studios that belong to this centre for creativity, culture, performance and exhibitions. The art wall below the old trains is one of the largest, most prominent and prestigious sites in the area for street art.

Overground Stations There are two new stations on the excellent Overground line, the building of which has contributed enormously to the rejuvenation of this part of London, and improved its connections to the rest of the city and beyond. Both were opened in 2010; there is the enormous, ultra-modern concrete box enlivened with stainless steel station at Shoreditch High Street where there's also a brand new viaduct, and the simple brick, glass and steel station at Hoxton with refurbished old arches that have been filled by businesses such as Fabrique Bakery (see page 26).

Truman pubs The history of beer-drinking and gathering in warm, sociable places is made clear on the streets of Shoreditch where, like any other densely populated, low-income inner city area, there were once pubs on practically every corner. Truman, Hanbury & Buxton was the local brewery; it was established in 1666 and the enormous buildings on Brick Lane which closed in 1989 are now venues for a mass of businesses, events, fairs, food stalls and night-time happenings which attract huge numbers, especially at weekends. Trumans also owned a large number of pubs, many of which were smartened up in the 1920s and 1930s with emerald green or chartreuse glazed brick exteriors with fancy, decorative lettering in faïence above. These splendid leftovers of East End boozer culture can be found all over Shoreditch: The Jolly Butchers on Brick Lane (now Brick Lane Coffee), the Dolphin on Redchurch Street (now Labour and Wait, see page 83), the empty Hop Pole on Pitfield Street, the still-thriving Royal Oak on Columbia Road (see page 79), and the Golden Heart on Commercial Street in Spitalfields which has a great Thirties interior and good examples of the very nice stained glass in simple designs with warm golds, ambers and yellows that appears in many Trumans pubs around London.

Find a
quiet spot

St Leonard's Church This is the Shoreditch church whose bells say 'when I get rich' in the nursery rhyme 'Oranges and Lemons' and it was once was the church where the prosperous families worshipped and displayed their wealth in front of the impoverished locals. Built in 1740 by George Dance the Elder, this tall, slim, elegant church with Doric portico and clear Italian influences is now one of the area's great landmarks and (with its Clerk's House next door) its oldest building. It's also where the BBC TV show 'Rev' was filmed, and unfortunately it's just as dilapidated in real life as it appears on screen. Inside it is very grand and crumbling but, while it might be lacking money, it's not short of atmosphere and drama. Despite the Victorians who made mistakes and bricked up the lower windows, this is still a wonderfully unadorned, un-refurbished interior, and an excellent link with and testimony to the past. The church does sterling work with people recovering from addictions and difficulties, and you can support it by getting your coffee at Paper and Cup across the road (page 69). There are lovely gardens on the sunny Calvert Avenue side with a mix of perennial and annual planting, including a colourful natural meadow area along the railings which, in summer, is full of pretty flowers.

(Inside it also has one of the weirdest monuments I have seen, an eighteenth-century memorial to Elizabeth Benson which shows two skeletons rending apart an oak tree with a line stretched between them from which hangs a sheet with an inscription in Latin. It is the horribly thin, dancing skeletons that surprise, but you have to admire the immense skill of Francis Bird, the man who carved it).

i USUALLY OPEN MON-FRI 12-2 MARCH-OCT, OR BY ARRANGEMENT

» 119 SHOREDITCH HIGH STREET SEE WEBSITE FOR CONTACT DETAILS

@ WWW.SHOREDITCHCHURCH.ORG.UK

St John's Church Unlike St Leonard's with its limited opening times, St John's in Hoxton can be visited very easily. This imposing, neo-classical Commissioners' church, built in 1826, was built by Francis Edwards, the foremost pupil of pupil of Sir John Soane. It is remarkable for its floor plan which has remained intact and unchanged, and for the notable ceiling painting by JA Reeve. The latter is stunning; it was created in the early twentieth-century and its intense azure background highlights the angels of the Apocalyse with their attractive, gentle, Arts & Crafts style faces. By contrast, the rest of the interior with galleries on three sides is still very Georgian, and is painted in a typical, genteel and elegant scheme of pale blue, white, and gold. The twentieth century is represented by some wonderful, colourful, storybook, post-war stained glass; the window with the children of all nations may be full of the type of primary school textbook stereotypes, but it is beautiful nonetheless, and contains what is probably the best pair of Mary Jane shoes you are ever likely to find immortalised in glass. Worth seeing, and can be combined with a tea/coffee stop at the Curious Yellow Kafe at 77 Pitfield Street.

i OPEN MON-FRI 7-5, SUN 9-1, CLOSED SAT

» PITFIELD STREET TEL 020 7739 9302

@ WWW.STJOHNSHOXTON.ORG.UK

Bunhill Fields It may not be everyone's choice of location to linger–although many do when it's sunny and warm – but Bunhill Fields is surely one of the most quietly atmospheric places in London. It's a well-used short-cut, but it's worth slowing down in here and considering the rich history. From 1655 to 1854 this was a burial ground, in particular for Nonconformists, and there are some very famous names here such as John Bunyan, Daniel Defoe, and William Blake, whose tombs and headstones can be located by looking at the map on the noticeboard. When the Victorians created large cemeteries further from the centre of London, it became a public park in 1869 (it is now much reduced from what it was). It has a nicely Gothic feel with foxgloves and creeping moss and, in more modern parlance, is a site of much prized urban biodiversity with crocuses, daffodils, London planes, oaks, limes and a black mulberry tree.

i OPEN APRIL-SEP MON-FRI 7.30-7 OR DUSK (WHICHEVER EARLIER),

SAT-SUN 9.30-7/DUSK, OCT-MARCH MON-FRI 7.30-4, SAT-SUN 9.30-4

▶ 38 CITY ROAD

@ WWW.ISLINGTON.GOV.UK

Wesley's Chapel Opposite Bunhill Fields is the chapel built in 1778 by George Dance the Younger for John Wesley. Wesley called it 'perfectly neat but not fine', but in fact this little-known architectural gem is actually very fine. It is a lovely Georgian building set back off the main road with an elegant courtyard and is now in great condition, thanks to extensive renovations in the 1970s. The interior is impressive and plain, a mix of pale colours and dark wood, but not dour or sombre. It is similar in layout to the other Georgian churches in Shoreditch - St

Leonard's and St John's - but is less resplendent and more restrained, as you would expect – although it is certainly not austere. This is a calm, quiet place in a busy part of London, and there are regular lunchtime piano or organ recitals (see website for details).

i OPEN MON-SAT 10-4, SUN SERVICE 12.30-1.45,
CLOSED THURS FOR SERVICE 12.30-1.45

⟩⟩ 49 CITY ROAD TEL 020 7253 2262

@ WWW.WESLEYCHAPEL.ORG.UK

The Garden at Geffrye Museum From the end of March to the end of October the gardens that surround the long, low frontage of the old almshouses are open and free to visit. The front garden is plain, formal and in keeping with the building, but to the side and behind are a group of period gardens (17th to 20th century) and a herb garden which are orderly and nicely planted with colourful flowers and aromatic plants. They provide an area of peacefulness sandwiched between the rumble of trains on one side and the noise of cars and buses on the other. See page 19 for contact details.

THIS PAGE *St John's Church*
OPPOSITE *Bunhill Fields*

See the patterns

There is plenty of evidence to suggest that people in Shoreditch like to impose a little order and beauty where they can with everyday objects. Everywhere you go, there are patterns, arrangements, stacks, lines, groups, and rows which make Shoreditch – an area without a significant architectural style - a visually interesting and dynamic place. Look, for example, at the incredible daily greengrocer displays at Yours Food Centre at 51-53 Pitfield Street, the cheerful rows of sunglasses and the stacks of bagels on Brick Lane, the tasteful, natural arrangements of fruit and veg at Leila's on Calvert Avenue, the gloriously colourful flowers on Columbia Road, the modern architectural patterns on Rivington Place, the stacks of Allpress cups on Redchurch Street, the book displays at Camden Lock Bookshop, and the fast-moving rows of sticky buns and pastries at Fabrique.

OPPOSITE *Veg display at Albion* FOLLOWING PAGES *Tiles on Shoreditch High Street and Flowers at Columbia Road Market*

Watch a film

With its mix of large local audiences and film buffs, Shoreditch is a prime spot for cinemas. It's a multiplex-free zone, and has two excellent but very different independent cinemas, and an informal cinema club which organises screenings of cultishly bad films. You can see everything from the latest blockbuster to the most recherché foreign-language, art house film.

Electric Cinema The Electric Cinema is run in conjunction with the club at Shoreditch House (see page 112) and those who are familiar with its sister cinema, the Electric Cinema on Portobello Road, will know to expect great comfort and style from this small 45-seat cinema. So there are squishy, velvet chairs and settees, warm blankets, padded footstools, drinks from the bar, and a mix of mainstream and art house films. It may be more expensive than some cinemas but it is not ridiculously so – in fact some of the big screens in the West End charge the same for a far less sybaritic cinema experience. The Electric feels like a first class airline cabin experience for a tiny fraction of the price.

i OPEN MON-SUN 12-9.30

▶ 64-66 REDCHURCH STREET TEL 020 3350 3490

@ WWW.ELECTRICCINEMA.CO.UK

Rich Mix The right name for this arts hub in central Shoreditch, which was opened in 2006 and is run as a charity and social enterprise. All audiences are catered for here with three screens - the largest one has a dramatic red and black décor, patterned panels inspired by the many local textile communities, and extremely comfortable seats. The programme has a 'rich mix' programme of major releases, shorts, documentaries, art house films, children's matinées and film seasons, with excellent ticket prices.

i OPEN MON-FRI 9-11, SAT-SUN 10-11

⟩ 34-47 BETHNAL GREEN ROAD TEL 020 7613 7498

@ WWW.RICHMIX.ORG.UK

See a crap film Indulge in the pleasure of enjoying a film you know to be execrable in the company of others who derive the same enjoyment from a terrible movie at one of the Book Club's Crap Film Club screenings.

⟩ 100-106 LEONARD STREET TEL 020 7684 8618

@ WWW.WEARETBC.COM

THIS PAGE *Camden Lock Books, Old Street Station*
OPPOSITE *Paper & Cup, Calvert Avenue*

PAPER & CUP

Pick up a book

It is always a huge pleasure nowadays to discover small, independent bookshops which are passionate about the printed word, and it's nice to see that Shoreditch has a good number. This means it's possible to follow your literary bent and at the same time help to keep enterprising bookshops alive by buying books or magazines from them.

Artwords A small, coolly white, totally excellent shop owned by a former Waterstones bookseller who fills it with shelves, tables, rows and piles of neatly arranged stacked books, periodicals, magazines on contemporary visual arts, fashion, art history and theory, photography, design, and architecture, many of which have been imported from Europe and America. It's a treat to find a bookshop which is unashamedly specialist without being exclusive. There are hard-to-find, obscure books mixed with well-known and classic titles from mainstream publishers. (There is second branch in London Fields.)

ⓘ OPEN MON-FRI 11-7, SAT 11-7, SUN 12-6

▶ 69 RIVINGTON STREET TEL 020 7729 2000

@ WWW.ARTWORDS.CO.UK

Material Material was set up in 2007 in Ludlow – this is the London outpost - as a gallery to represent designers and artists from a variety of visual disciplines, and as a bookshop to offer affordable limited edition prints. This is an elegant, tall, beautifully arranged room with a mix of books, periodicals, stationery, prints and cards which have clearly been chosen with taste and care. The books are mostly creative, arty and illustrated, and there are stylish travel guides and cookery titles, too. You are guaranteed to find something here that you haven't seen elsewhere, or the perfect book or printed gift for a friend.

i OPEN MON-FRI 11-7, SAT 11-6

➤ 3 RIVINGTON STREET TEL 0207 739 1900

@ WWW.MATERIALMATERIAL.COM

Brick Lane Bookshop Squeezed in amongst the old Truman brewery buildings, the vintage shops, the bagels, the cafés and the curry houses on one of London's most characterful streets is this brilliant bookshop. It has been supplying readers in the East End for thirty years with carefully selected books and, as the bookshop isn't huge, the intelligent selection is what it's all about. It's particularly strong on local and London history and guides - if there's a London or East End book worth having, it will be here - but it's also good for classics, children's books, travel, and poetry.

i OPEN 11-6.30 DAILY

➤ 66 BRICK LANE TEL 020 7247 0216

@ WWW.BRICKLANEBOOKSHOP.ORG

Paper and Cup A tiny, cosy café that brings together two of life's greatest small pleasures - coffee and books – with the aim of helping others. Paper and Cup is a not-for-profit, social enterprise café created and run by the Spitalfields Crypt Trust. The coffee comes, as you would hope, in paper cups with a nice, distinctive design, and there are new and second-hand books for sale. The tables are small but this is a good place to drink your coffee, enjoy fresh cake or a brownie, pick up a book, buy bag of beans, and help a charity all at the same time.

i OPEN MON-FRI 8-6, SAT 9-6, SUN 10-5

▶ 18 CALVERT AVENUE TEL 020 7739 5358

@ WWW.PAPERANDCUP.CO.UK

Camden Lock Books The best station bookshop I know. In the past, Old Street tube station would probably be very low on any list of popular tube and railway stations, but its warren of passages and confusion of exits under the huge roundabout are now being turned into an interesting retail experience where you can pick up coffee or hot soup, buy a bunch of flowers, and browse for books in the brilliant Camden Lock Books. It's been here since 2005, although the shop started in Camden Lock Market in 1984, hence the name. It has excellent general stock (with a mix of full and discounted prices) and good photography, art and local sections plus a great selection of postcards. The manager, Jason, is very knowledgeable, the location is amazingly convenient, and it's really worth missing a train or two to find a classic for your journey.

i OPEN MON-FRI 8.30-7, SAT 12-5, CLOSED SUN

▶ OLD STREET STATION TEL 020 7253 0666

@ WWW.CAMDENLOCKBOOKS.COM

Book Art Bookshop Round the corner from Old Street station is this tiny, very red, specialist bookshop which sells artists' books and small press publications – many of which call into question and play with the concept and form of the book in highly imaginative and creative ways. Its stock comes directly from artists and from independent publishers (such as the excellent Redstone Press) which the owner thinks will interest the 'aesthetically and bibliographically curious' and offer a very different and thought-provoking take on the book. There are also lectures, events, discussions, and workshops.

i OPEN WEDS-FRI 1-7, SAT 12-6 (CLOSED AUGUST, CHRISTMAS & NEW YEAR)

CHECK TIMES IN ADVANCE AS LAST-MINUTE CHANGES CAN HAPPEN

▶ 17 PITFIELD STREET TEL 020 7608 1333

@ WWW.BOOKARTBOOKSHOP.COM

THIS PAGE *Subsidence,*
St Luke's Church
OPPOSITE *Lupins,*
Columbia Road

Have a
special Sunday

Shoreditch is good any day of the week, but it's particularly brilliant on a Sunday. You may want to plan ahead for a special Sunday, or simply turn up and have a spontaneously good one. Combine breakfast or brunch with flowers, treats and cake, browsing and shopping, and round off with a huge, old-fashioned Sunday roast in a pub, or a lighter lunch in one of Shoreditch's many good eating places.

SUNDAY BREAKFAST There is every kind of Sunday breakfast, from light and fast to full and slow, available in and around Shoreditch. Go to Beigel Bake on Brick Lane for a bag of bagels, or to Albion for the newspapers with a civilised breakfast, or have fried eggs at Leila's, tea and cake at Vintage Heaven, or an open-air coffee and a pastry in the courtyard of the Royal Oak, or at one of the many little cafés and coffee spots on and around Columbia Road.

SUNDAY FLOWERS The Columbia Road flower market is the brightly coloured and characterful magnet that pulls in the crowds to this part of London on a Sunday. You know when you are getting close when you see people staggering away with enormous bunches of flowers, tall plants in pots, and massive sheaves of foliage. The market is not huge but what it lacks in length, it makes up in sheer volume of flowers and plants. It is packed with wonderful displays and buckets and boxes and bunches of huge bunches of mostly seasonal flowers in fabulous colour combinations, sold by old-fashioned market traders whose cries gets louder and more competitive as the morning progresses (the prices drop over time or in poor and wet weather). Buying can be a bit of a gamble and not everything lasts very well, but there can be some great seasonal bargains such as peonies, tulips, Isles of Scilly narcissi, delphiniums, roses, sunflowers, potted hyacinths, and it's also worth looking at vegetable seedlings and herb plants. At peak time (mid to late morning) it can be a terrible squash, but it's all done with good humour. Take carrier bags or big IKEA-style bags to hold purchases.

i OPEN SUNDAY ONLY, 8 TO 3-ISH

▶ COLUMBIA ROAD

@ WWW.COLUMBIAROAD.INFO

SUNDAY SHOPPING AND SUNDAY TREATS To think it's not so long ago that Sunday shopping was unheard of in this country, yet at Columbia Road there is Sunday-only shopping. Although a few shops have extended their hours to include Saturdays, Sunday is still the main trading day because of the flower market. The road, which seems not to have altered for a century or so, is lined with little shops that have these limited opening times such as Rob Ryan, Vintage Heaven, Suck and Chew, A Portuguese Love Affair, Keeping Choosing Stationery, Angela Flanders, although businesses come and go, which means you might discover that a recommended or favourite place has disappeared seemingly overnight. The best advice is to wander around, up and down, in and out, and you are bound to come across something lovely and unusual.

Lily Vanilli The Lily Vanilli bakery-café is tiny but manages to cram in many very nice cakes which look lovely *and* taste delicious, and people to eat them. The eponymous Lily is also a cake designer with high-powered client list, and author of the delectable *Sweet Tooth* (2012). I go for the cherry bakewell cakes, the cherry almond friands, and the wonderful plump sausage rolls which you can smell a long way off. Eat in or take away.

i OPEN SUN 8.30-4

⟩ 6 THE COURTYARD, EZRA STREET

@ WWW.LILYVANILLI.COM

Suck and Chew Give yourself some 'spends' (pocket money) on a Sunday and choose a bag of sweets at Suck and Chew, a small family business in lovely little scarlet shop with an enticing window on Columbia Road. It's only open on flower market day (you can also buy online) which means that buying bonbons, toffee, liquorice, humbugs, pear drops and so on here is a special treat. You'll find all the sweet shop favourites shaken out of a jar and weighed by hand, just as they should be.

i OPEN SUN 9-4, OR BUY FROM THE WEBSITE

⟩ 130 COLUMBIA ROAD TEL 020 8983 3504

@ WWW.SUCKANDCHEW.CO.UK

Vintage Heaven and Cakehole There's enough vintage/retro stuff in here to keep any lover of old china, glass, home wares, fabrics and bits and pieces happy. The huge amount of china is displayed by colour which is a lovely – and very tempting - way to show it off. This is a great place for a Sunday rummage plus a cup of tea and slice of coffee and walnut cake in the 50s style Cakehole café (lots of framed, old needle-point pictures and old-fashioned counter displays). The cream teas are a fine Sunday treat with scones baked in Stepney, jam from Borough Market, and tea from Greenwich.

i OPEN FRI BY APPOINTMENT, SAT 12-6, SUN 8.30-5.50

CAKEHOLE OPEN SAT 11-5, SUN 8.30-5

82 COLUMBIA ROAD TEL 01277 215968

@ WWW.VINTAGEHEAVEN.CO.UK

SUNDAY LUNCH Princess of Shoreditch On Sundays, the Princess of Shoreditch goes all out on roasts with a deliciously hearty Pickwickian menu in suitably old premises done up in with charm and style. The characterful, smart pub is in a 270 year old building which combines pale, elegant, Georgian structure with solid, dark Edwardian furniture, making it a lovely place to sit and take your time over Sunday lunch and good wine (the list is excellent). If you haven't booked a table in the pricier upstairs dining room where reservations are advised, light dishes such as fried anchovies, radishes, scotch eggs and mussels are served in the pub downstairs. A traditional East End boozer it is not.

i OPEN MON-SAT 12-11, SUN 12-10.30

(KITCHEN OPEN MON-FRI 12-3 AND 6.30-10.30, SAT 12-4 AND 6-10, SUN 12-9)

76-78 PAUL STREET TEL 020 7729 9270

@ WWW.THEPRINCESSOFSHOREDITCH.COM

Boundary In the basement of the 1893 warehouse building which now contains a hotel and Albion (page 36) is the more formal Boundary restaurant, which does a very good *prix-fixe* Sunday menu and the kind of good French bourgeois cooking you would expect of a *dimanche* in a smart restaurant in the provinces of France. On Sundays, the menu concentrates on Sunday lunch classics such as oysters, *fruits de mer* and home-made *charcuterie* served from a trolley (highly recommended), *daube de bœuf*, and treats such as a soufflé or *crème brûlée*.

i OPEN MON-SAT 6.30-10.30, SUN LUNCH 12-4

❯❯ 2-4 BOUNDARY STREET (ENTRANCE ON REDCHURCH STREET) TEL 020 7729 1051

@ WWW.BOUNDARY.CO.UK

Owl and Pussycat The Owl and Pussycat is in a former pub which has been opened up, stripped back to brick and old paint, filled with bashed leather settees, pieces of mid-century furniture, and flowers in jam jars, to create a carefully managed downbeat look. It keeps things simple with Big Apple Hot Dogs, locally sourced ingredients, and a nicely traditional, unfancy Sunday roast lunch with roasted everything, including a vegetarian option, and old-fashioned, sticky, filling puddings. If you don't want to go for the full Sunday lunch, it is still good for a beer and something small, a hot dog, or burger with chips.

i OPEN MON 12-11, SAT 12-12, SUN 12-11 (SUNDAY LUNCH FROM 12 UNTIL ALL GONE), UPSTAIRS SNUG BAR OPEN MON-FRI FROM 6, SAT-SUN FROM MIDDAY). BIG APPLE HOT DOGS DAILY 12-12

❯❯ 34 REDCHURCH STREET TEL 020 3487 0088

@ WWW.OWLANDPUSSYCATSHOREDITCH.COM

The Royal Oak Pub Surrounded by the bustle, blooms and cries of Columbia Road flower market is this 1920s Truman's pub with glazed tile exterior, made-to-last tiled lettering, and very plain, spit 'n' sawdust interior. It makes a fine retreat from the market; a nip of whisky or a cup of Climpson coffee may just the thing to defrost fingers on bitter winter days. On Sundays, there is a café in the courtyard (access via the laneway behind the pub) where you can get coffee, Brick Lane bagels, and pastries between 9 and 2, and the upstairs dining room (12-4) does fish and chips, chicken, steak, and sticky toffee pudding. It's a real crush in here on Sundays but it's all part of the market atmosphere.

i OPEN MON-FRI 4-11, SAT-SUN 12-11

DINING ROOM OPEN TUES-SAT 7-10, SUN 12-4

73 COLUMBIA ROAD TEL 020 78729 2220

@ WWW.ROYALOAKLONDON.COM WWW.ABOVETHEOAK.COM

THIS PAGE *Truman pub stained glass*
OPPOSITE *Crescent Trading*

Shop for useful
and beautiful things

The proprietors of long-established, old-time, down-to-earth Shoreditch businesses must be a little bemused by the comings and goings of the new wave of high-end shops in the area. Retail can be a precarious way to make a living, and shops here can appear and disappear in the blink of an eye, with regular movement, changes, and closures. The ones that stay the course such as Labour and Wait, Luna and Curious, Cowling & Wilcox, Leila's and Ally Cappellino are those that have a range of prices, a timeless quality, a fairly wide market, and are backed by a very definite personality or group of people. With so many creative, independent shopkeepers, Shoreditch is currently a great place to shop; it is a world away from the high street, and blessedly free of the big international luxury brands. Instead, you'll find all sorts of interesting little places with carefully chosen stock, which have made Shoreditch into a kind of showcase of good, often British, design and craftsmanship, of beautiful, useful, well-made things. They mark a return to valuing traditional manufacturing methods and quality, an approach that fits in well the area's long history of workshops and small-scale manufacturing.

Redchurch Street, Rivington Street and Calvert Avenue are the best shopping streets. In addition to the shops mentioned below, smart places include APC, Aida, House of Hackney Hostem, Religion, Denham, and Start (if they are still there when you visit – if not, an equally hip business will no doubt be *in situ*).

HARDWARE AND GROCERIES Labour and Wait The first, the best, and still unrivalled in the category of shops which sell you items that you don't know you need until you see them and then realise they are absolutely fit for purpose: timeless and functional objects such as twine, feather dusters, bottle brushes, pocket flasks, and proper pencil sharpeners which last for ages. Labour and Wait was established in 2000 and is now in one of the many gloriously green-tiled former Truman pubs in the area – this used to be The Dolphin (see page 48). The owners track down specialist manufacturers, many of whom still use original designs and methods, and the shop is a kind of retail museum of beautifully made stuff such as soap from Portugal, brushes from Germany, enamel kettles from Japan, Brown Betty teapots from Staffordshire, giant aluminium dust pans from America, potting trowels from Holland, and string bags from France.

i OPEN TUES-SUN 11-6, CLOSED MON

▶ 85 REDCHURCH STREET TEL 020 7729 6253

@ WWW.LABOURANDWAIT.CO.UK

Leila's Leila's grocery is an amazing place which honours and celebrates seasonality, with a proprietor who undertakes to find the best of what's available from a network of suppliers or via market trips. Customers are best advised to leave any shopping list at home, and to come instead to find out what's available because you can be sure it will be totally fresh and good. It's a world away from supermarket shopping, with lovely surprises, wonderful seasonal discoveries, delicacies such as Malaga raisins on the vine, Coleman coffee beans, the best fruit and veg you could wish for, from the ordinary and homely to the unusual and

THIS PAGE *Leila's, Calvert Avenue*

hard-to-find. Outside is an ever-changing display done with artistic simplicity and clear devotion to the beauty of greengrocery, and inside is a cool, shadowy Aladdin's cave of tins, bottles, tins, jars, boxes, baskets, racks and pile of cured meats, cheeses, breads, nuts, preserves, pastas, coffee and books. A dream grocer's such as this does not come cheap, but it's hard not to leave without something small such as a plump violet garlic, a couple of Sicilian lemons, or a loaf of sourdough.

i OPEN WEDS-SAT 10-6, SUN 10-5, CLOSED MON-TUES

▶ 15-17 CALVERT AVENUE   TEL 020 7729 9789

@ FACEBOOK PAGE AND TWITTER

Albion Customers arriving at Albion are always greeted by two small but colourful and creative displays of fresh, seasonal fruit and veg, one on either side of the door. They set the tone for a well-stocked grocery/bakery which manages to cover pretty much all you'd need for a meal at any time of the day. It has a particularly good selection of baked goods (a full cake table, trays of fresh pastries and breakfast buns, boxes of bread) which come directly from the kitchen, and shelves of traditional condiments, and jars of flavoursome jams and marmalade made in London by England Preserves (see page 36 for details).

CLOTHES AND ACCESSORIES Present A 'contemporary retail space' ('shop', you could say) which specialises in menswear and also brews a good cup of coffee. It's not obligatory to dress like the local hipsters, but if you want to, Present would be a good place to buy the necessary knitted striped tops, heavy lace-up shoes and Lyle and Scott polo shirts. However, it also stocks many well-made extras and eclectic accessories such as books, watch straps, loudly patterned swim shorts, fantastic socks, smart belts and a selection of Hikaru Noguchi knitted ties – and you don't have to be a member of any particular style group to like those. It's a nice mix: coffee, clothes, and creative window displays in an old shop whose front still claims it is 'The Golden Horn Cigarette Company'.

i OPEN MON-FRI 10.30-7, SAT 11-6.30, SUN 11-5

❯❯ 140 SHOREDITCH HIGH STREET   TEL 020 7033 0500

@ WWW.PRESENT-LONDON.COM

MHL This was the first shop for MHL, Margaret Howell's second, sportier, (allegedly) more affordable label, and is a haven for tidy people who find neatness calming and therapeutic - everything is perfectly aligned and folded, and there is not a collar or crease out of place. If funds permit, come here for MH's pared down, high quality, classic look and the perfect capsule wardrobe of dark wool trousers, white cotton shirt, cashmere sweater, and twill jacket. Or just enjoy the ultra-plain display and enviably effortless look.

i OPEN MON-SAT 10-7, SUN 12-5

❯❯ 19 OLD NICHOL STREET   TEL 020 7033 9494

@ WWW.MARGARETHOWELL.CO.UK

Tracey Neuls Tracey Neuls makes beautiful shoes in lovely colours with distinctively shaped toes and heels that make them look like something out of the *Wizard of Oz*. The shoes in this tiny shop hang down from the ceiling in a shoe cloud, a clever way of allowing customers to get a good all-round view.

i OPEN TUES-SUN 11-6, CLOSED MON

▶ 73 REDCHURCH STREET TEL 020 7018 0872

@ WWW.TRACEYNEULS.COM

Milk In the small, narrow, eighteenth century Clerk's House squeezed in right next door to St Leonard's Church is Milk, a 'concept boutique' which focusses on homeware, furniture and clothes, internationally recognised designers, new collections and emerging talent. Although it's beyond the average budget, it's good to see an old building housing a new business.

i OPEN MON-FRI 11-7, SAT 11-6, SUN 12-5

▶ 118 Ð SHOREDITCH HIGH STREET TEL 020 7729 9880

@ WWW.MILKCONCEPTBOUTIQUE.CO.UK

Sunspel Sunspel has been producing classic boxers since the 1940s (Nick Kamen wore a white pair in the famous 1980s Levi's advert set in a launderette), and has manufactured underwear and T-shirts since it was founded in Nottingham in 1860. It was bought in 2005 and has been turned into a classic British brand still with the focus on simple clothing made from beautiful fabrics - at a price, though. Maybe buy a pair of classic boxers for old times' sake.

ⓘ OPEN MON-SAT 11-7, SUN & BANK HOLS 12-5

▶ 5 AND 7 REDCHURCH STREET TEL 020 7739 9729

@ WWW.SUNSPEL.COM

Luna and Curious A treasure trove of carefully chosen stock, this shop is run as a collective by three designers whose magpie tendencies and good taste bring together a delightful mix of unusual jewellery, ceramics, accessories and other eye-catching discoveries. The nail varnishes, tights, mugs, witty jewellery, magazines, and fabulous Bonne Maison socks from France which are mini works of textile art (not cheap, but amazing) are my top picks.

ⓘ OPEN MON-SAT 11-6, SUN 11-5

▶ 24-26 CALVERT AVENUE TEL 020 3222 0034

@ WWW.LUNAANDCURIOUS.COM

Ally Cappellino is known for her well-made, practical bags for both men and women, and her plain, high-quality look fits in perfectly here on Calvert Avenue. The bags and accessories are simple in shape and detailing, and are made from top quality materials such as Italian leather and English waxed cotton. These are very understated statement bags, satchels, totes and rucksacks which are made to do a job rather than just hang from an arm.

ⓘ OPEN MON-SAT 11-6, SUN 11-5

▶ 9 CALVERT AVENUE TEL 020 7033 7843

@ WWW.ALLYCAPPELLINO.CO.UK

Aesop Aesop on Redchurch Street is part of an Australian company which makes skin, hair and beauty products. Each store is breathtakingly neat with ultra-minimal product displays, which makes them look like a cross between Damien Hirst's pharmacies and a real laboratory. The white and black shop in Shoreditch is austere - so bare it's barely there - with a seriously pared down look, and the result is high-minded yet seductive.

i OPEN MON 11-6, TUES-FRI 11-7, SAT 10-6, SUN 11-5

▶ 5A REDCHURCH STREET TEL 020 7613 3793

@ WWW.AESOP.COM

PENS, PAPERS, PAINTS Keeping Choosing A wonderful little stationery store, and a fresh, modern version of what used to be delightful but rather stuffy, old-fashioned places. The French owner brings together a great collection of the best bits and pieces from around the world. Extremely desirable things include beautiful Sakura Coupy Pencils from Japan in a tin with a design that hasn't changed since 1973, handmade Astier de Villatte diaries from France with lovely tile patterns on the covers, useful all-weather Alwych notebooks from Scotland ('made to withstand even the Scottish weather'), letterpress cards and bookplates, and little bottles of glue from Germany.

i OPEN WEDS-SAT 11.30-7, SUN 9.30-5, CLOSED MON & TUES

▶ 128 COLUMBIA ROAD TEL 020 7613 3842

@ WWW.CHOOSINGKEEPING.COM

Cowling & Wilcox This well-known company, which supplies artists with all they need, opened its Shoreditch branch around ten years ago when it noticed the increase in artistic and creative types in the area. If nothing else, it's worth going in for drawing inks by Winsor & Newton. These have been used by illustrators since the 1890s, and are sold in lovely tiny boxes which are miracles of packaging design with illustrations relating to the colour of the ink in the box.

ℹ OPEN MON-SAT 9.30-6.30, SUN 11.30-5.30

⟩ 112 SHOREDITCH HIGH STREET TEL 020 7033 3685

@ WWW.COWLINGANDWILCOX.COM

FABRICS Crescent Trading The East End has always played a big role in London's rag trade, but nowadays there are few traders and tailors left, and it's certainly not as easy as it was to find really good wool suiting and high quality fabrics for garments. Crescent Trading maintains the tradition, though, and has a large, utilitarian warehouse full of bolts and rolls of fine, mostly British fabrics, and is particularly good for woollens and 'Finest English Suitings', the type that has 'Woven in Huddersfield' on the selvedge. There are no price tags, so you need to ask one of the two dapper gentlemen owners who are suitably elegantly besuited and who know all the fabrics, fibres, and factories. Many of the fabrics are end-of-line rolls, so buy what you like and/or need when you see it.

ℹ OPEN MON-THURS 9.30-5, FRI 9.30-2, CLOSED SAT, SUN 9-2

⟩ UNIT 2, QUAKER COURT, 41 QUAKER STREET TEL 020 7377 5067

@ WWW.CRESCENTTRADING.COM

The Shop Brick Lane is a haven for vintage enthusiasts but The Shop stands out because of its vast stock. It has lots of vintage clothing, particularly womenswear, and the front room is packed with vintage fabrics, textiles (tablecloths, handkerchiefs, scarves, curtains, aprons, tea towels) and bits of haberdashery such as buttons. It's a good place to rummage and the prices are fair. While you are there, Cheshire Street has some interesting and creative businesses, and good street art (look also at Blackmans Yard which is a little way up on the right as you walk away from Brick Lane).

𝑖 OPEN MON-SAT 11-6, SUN 9.30-5

⟩ 3 CHESHIRE STREET TEL 020 7739 5631

OPPOSITE *Wall of colour*

THIS PAGE *Crescent Trading*
OPPOSITE *Ace Hotel clock*

Go by bike

As you might expect, Shoreditch is not short of smart, specialist cycling businesses. It is also the centre of the less legal trade in 'second-hand' bikes on Sunday mornings at Brick Lane Market, the place to go to haggle or perhaps to find your missing bike.

Brick Lane Bikes Not quite on Brick Lane, but just round the corner on Bethnal Green Road. Brick Lane Bikes is a workshop and shop which sells its own BLB components, many beautiful vintage bikes, track and road bikes, and all the necessary cycling kit.

i OPEN MON-FRI 9-7, SAT 11-6, SUN 11-5

▶ 118 BETHNAL GREEN ROAD TEL 020 7033 9053

@ WWW.BRICKLANEBIKES.CO.UK

Tokyobike is a small, independent company set up in Tokyo in 2002, selling beautiful, colourful, streamlined, form-follows-function bikes which were designed to suit cycling in Tokyo. They are modern and at the same time nicely traditional, very desirable, and not cheap. Test rides are offered, and it is possible to hire a bike for a day, which would be a perfectly fitting way to get around Shoreditch. It's best to contact the store in advance – if you hire, they can supply a helmet and a lock, too.

i OPEN TUES-FRI 11-7, SAT-SUN 11-5

▶ 87-89 TABERNACLE STREET TEL 020 3239 2311

@ WWW.TOKYOBIKE.CO.UK

'Boris' Bikes Check the TFL website for details of where to find 'Boris Bike' stands in and around Shoreditch (there is a stand on Shoreditch High Street and another outside Hoxton station), and take one along canal towpath to Towpath Café (see page 106). www.tfl.gov.uk/modes/cycling/barclays-cycle-hire

Do something
different

Have a traditional wet shave Shoreditch has an extremely high concentration of beards which require maintenance, hence the appearance of self-consciously old-fashioned barbers such as Murdock which now has six branches in London. The Shoreditch one is on Redchurch Street, close to all the other services and products a gentleman needs to maintain a hipster look and lifestyle. They do wet shaves and moustache trims and beard reshaping with cut-throat razors, they cut hair into the latest style, and also sell their own label, British-made male grooming products and accessories.

ⓘ OPEN MON-FRI 9-8, SAT 9-7, SUN 10-6

▶ 46 REDCHURCH STREET RESERVATIONS: TEL 0203 393 7946 OR BOOK ONLINE

@ WWW.MURDOCKLONDON.COM

Screenprint a t-shirt or watch a crap film Book Club is bookish in name only, and is a popular meeting place with large, interesting rooms in an old Victorian warehouse (think smart mid-century modern meets student union). It's undoubtedly young but the timetable of creative workshops (eg screenprinting T-shirts), talks, and mind-expanding events and its wonderfully named 'Crap Film Club' has a wide appeal. Foodwise, the Book Club day starts early with good breakfasts (served 8-12 Mon-Fri) and all-day brunches at the weekend (served Sat-Sun 10-5), moves through the day with changes in menus, and carries on all evening with informal evening classes, platters and bites and, for those with stamina, late-night drinking.

i OPEN MON-WEDS 8AM-12AM, THURS-FRI 8AM-12AM, SAT 10AM-2AM, SUN 10AM-12AM

❱❱ 100-106 LEONARD STREET TEL 020 7684 8618

@ WWW.WEARETBC.COM

Shop in a container Boxpark is a pop-up shopping centre with a difference: stripped and refitted shipping containers are stacked like children's building blocks to create an unusual retail environment. It's right next to Shoreditch High Street station and, so far, has shown good staying power with plenty of interesting small businesses (fashion, cafes, food, sport, hair) as well as some larger brands who want to squeeze in and have a presence here. The innovative MOO Printing has a box (Unit 27) where you can order business and other cards, as does Dum Dum Donutterie (Unit 31) which sells extremely inventive, extremely delicious, baked - rather than fried - doughnuts.

i FOOD AND DRINK SHOPS OPEN MON-SAT 8-11, SUN 10-10

FASHION SHOPS OPEN MON-SAT 11-7 EXCEPT THURS 11-8, SUN 12-6

❱❱ 2-10 BETHNAL GREEN ROAD TEL 0207 033 2899

@ WWW.BOXPARK.CO.UK

Eat/buy fresh pasta Shoreditch has its very own *pastaficio* on Redchurch Street where golden-yellow pasta is made daily, and can be bought to take home and cook or eaten on the premises in the tiny, white dining room at the back. Burro e Salvia ('butter and sage' – the name tells you all you need to know about the good, simple ingredients) has a short all-day menu of salads and breads and puddings, but the time to come for pasta is lunch (daily, 12-3) or dinner (Thurs-Sat, 7pm and 9pm sittings, booking advised) – a chance to enjoy fresh ravioli or tortellini with that rare beast: a bottle of proper, serious Lambrusco.

i OPEN MON-SAT 11-7, SUN 11-5

▷ 52 REDCHURCH STREET TEL 020 7739 4429

@ WWW.BURROESALVIA.CO.UK

Play table tennis As summer approaches, table tennis tables pop up all over London in public spots and are free to use – just bring your own bat and ball. One of the best locations of all is under the bandstand at the top of the mound in Arnold Circus which has a lovely view down Calvert Avenue and is conveniently close to coffee and brownies at Leila's (see page 37) or breakfast at Albion (see page 36). For all-year-round indoor ping pong with plenty of people ready and waiting to be challenged, go to the tables at the Book Club at 100 Leonard Street where bats and balls can be borrowed for free.

Have a hot drink at a tea stall Syd's Coffee Stall has been selling hot drinks and refreshments from its spot at the Shoreditch High Street end of Calvert Avenue since 1919. Stalls like this were once common all over London serving tea and coffee and saveloy, but have now all but disappeared. Syd's survives partly due to the high quality of the original mahogany, glass and brass stall, and partly due to the determination of Syd's granddaughter who runs the stall today. Syd's has been a literal fixture for a long time (see the cobbles underneath and the yellow parking line which skirts it which show that it was simply easier to work round it than to move it) but the rise of café culture all around now threatens it. At dusk on a cold winter's day, there are few more atmospheric places in London to go for a cup of tea, and imagine you're in a period black and white film.

i CORNER OF SHOREDITCH HIGH STREET AND CALVERT AVENUE, OPENING TIMES ARE ERRATIC

Eat Vietnamese food South of the Geffrye Museum, Kingsland Road has a cluster of Vietnamese restaurants which have given rise to the nickname 'Pho Mile'. Try fresh, fragrant, spicy and authentic dishes such as pho (noodle soup), pancakes, salads, spring rolls and rice dishes. Recommended places include Viet Grill at 58, Tay Do Café at 65, Viet Hoa Café and Mess at 70-72, Mien Tay at 122. Most open for lunch and dinner and close in between.

Learn to hula hoop... The historic Shoreditch Town Hall (1866, extended 1900s) is the place to go for hula hooping classes and tea dances and lots of often offbeat contemporary arts and culture. It has a splendid, grand assembly hall (it dates from 1907 and looks like the inside of a huge, pale, pink and gold shell) plus several smaller but equally interesting rooms and atmospheric spaces which are used for events, performances, launches and photoshoots.

➤ 380 OLD STREET TEL 020 7739 6176
@ WWW.SHOREDITCHTOWNHALL.COM

...or acquire circus skills If you've always wanted to fly through the air on a trapeze or walk a tightrope, in Shoreditch it's never too late to learn. In the huge generating and combustion chambers of the former Electric Light Station, the National Centre for Circus Arts offers 'experience days' and short courses in various circus skills to the general public and you don't need to have any previous experience or be particularly bendy to do one.

i OPEN MON-FRI 9-10, SAT-SUN 10-6

▶ CORONET STREET TEL 020 7613 4141

@ WWW.NATIONALCIRCUS.ORG.UK

Pick a perfume Although it's now something of an open secret, the beautifully old-fashioned Angela Flanders fragrance shop on Columbia Road still only opens on a Sunday, and can be incorporated into a morning of lovely floral scents and aromas. Everything is created by Angela Flanders, a former costume designer who knows how to put things together, and the character and individuality of her products make them very desirable in a world of international luxury brands. If you aren't in Shoreditch on a Sunday, there is a second shop in Spitalfields which is open seven days a week.

i OPEN SUN 10-4, SAT BY APPOINTMENT (PHONE THE SHOP)

   96 COLUMBIA ROAD TEL 020 7739 7555

   OPEN MON-FRI 11-6.30, SAT-SUN 11-5

▶ 4 ARTILLERY PASSAGE IN SPITALFIELDS TEL 020 7247 7040

@ WWW.ANGELAFLANDERS-PERFUMER.COM

Eat traditional eel, pie and mash A comma is often missing in the signs, which could lead you to think you'll be getting 'eel pie and mash', when in fact what's on offer is 'eel, pie and mash', all of which are options at F. Cooke, one of the few remaining traditional pie and mash houses in East London. This is true Cockney food; cheap, tasty, filling, and unpretentious. The surroundings are typical of this type of eating place: spartan white tiles, mirrors, marble table tops, benches, and the service is typically chatty and friendly. Pie is served with mash and a ladleful of green 'liquor' (a parsley sauce), or try the East End specialities of jellied eels or eel and mash. If you come on a Saturday, you'll be surrounded by the bustle of the market and the loyal locals who ensure places like this survive.

ⓘ OPEN MON-THURS 10-7, FRI-SAT 9.30-8, CLOSED SUN

》 150 HOXTON STREET TEL 020 7729 7718

Have your photo taken in a photobooth So what if it's old hat and teenagerish to squash into a tiny booth and pose for four small black and white photos, it's also great fun and the results are quick. No wonder old-style booths are appearing again, and this time it's not in department stores and railway stations but in bars, cafés and hotels. Commemorate a visit to Shoreditch in the booth in the lobby of the Ace Hotel or the booth which is under Pizza East and near the Concrete bar in the basement of the TEA building.

ⓘ ACE HOTEL, 100 SHOREDITCH HIGH STREET

》 PIZZA EAST AND CONCRETE, 56 SHOREDITCH HIGH STREET

THIS PAGE *Bethnal Green Road market*
OPPOSITE *Posters*

Syd's

THE ORIGINAL COFFEE STALL
Established here 1919
wish to thank all our Customers
past and present for supporting our
historic East End — landmark

HILLARY CATERERS
0181 346
4764 ••• FOR ALL OCCASIONS

Beyond and around Shoreditch

The following places are not quite in Shoreditch but they are within walking distance and definitely worth adding to an itinerary.

NORTH Canal and Towpath Café The Regent's Canal towpath is a great way to see the back of London, so to speak, as it cuts through the urban landscape and affords a new perspective, one you won't see from a pavement or car or bus or train. The canal stretches from Paddington in the west to Limehouse in the east and passes many landmarks on its way. The stretch north of Shoreditch isn't the most attractive section, but the towpath is still a quiet place for a walk, run or bike ride, and you can combine an activity with coffee/cake/brunch/snack stop at the Towpath Café – or just sit and watch others doing the walking, running and cycling. The café caused ripples along the canal when it opened and although several more cafés have arrived, the now-extended Towpath is still extremely popular and extremely good.

ⓘ OPEN TUES-WED 8-8, THURS-FRI 8-9, SAT-SUN 9AM-11PM, CLOSED MON (CHECK FACEBOOK PAGE FOR CURRENT TIMES)

▶ 36 DE BEAUVOIR CRESCENT (ON THE NORTH SIDE OF THE CANAL BETWEEN THE KINGSLAND ROAD BRIDGE AND THE WHITMORE ROAD BRIDGE) TEL 020 7254 7606

@ FACEBOOK PAGE 'TOWPATH CAFÉ'

SOUTH WEST Barbican Less than a mile from Shoreditch High Street and right in the heart of the City of London is the Barbican, a must-see if you have any interest in modern architecture, culture, Brutalism and/or concrete. The Barbican Estate was built on bomb-damaged land to provide housing for four thousand residents, and although it was officially opened in 1969, building carried on through the Seventies. The whole thing is a phenomenal design and construction by Chamberlin, Powell and Moya, and it's hard not to be impressed by the size and scale of the towers and the vast landscaped inner courtyards which resemble the Hanging Gardens of Babylon. Next to these is the Barbican Centre (opened 1983), an absolutely huge arts centre with an enormous hall, theatre, three screens, a library, a gallery and various bars and restaurants. The gallery has some of the most interesting, cutting-edge and thought-provoking exhibitions in London, although it's worth coming to the Centre anyway to be overawed by the almost Soviet scale of ambition, planning, and space. The best place to have a drink, sandwich or meal here is the buzzing, relaxed Foodhall on level G (Mon-Sat 9-8, Sun, 11-8) which also has tables outside.

There is a really useful 'Discover the Barbican' walking guide that allows you to take a self-guided tour (available at the Barbican or download from the Barbican website). The Barbican also has a programme of Architecture Tours (check website for times).

i BARBICAN CENTRE OPEN MON-SAT 9-11, SUN 10-11, BANK HOLIDAYS 12-11

ART GALLERY OPEN SUN-WED 10-6, THURS-FRI 10-9, CLOSED SUN

▶ SILK STREET TEL 020 7638 8891

@ WWW.BARBICAN.ORG.UK

EAST Classic café E. Pellicci, just under half a mile from the top of Brick Lane, is a famous East London landmark, a fully preserved greasy spoon with fabulous frontage and fittings which date from 1946 (the café has been here since 1900) and is still run by the same family. The chrome and Vitrolite exterior and incredible café interior are Grade II listed, and put most modern caffs to shame. Because it has not been altered, its post-war 'utilitarian meets Art Deco' style is all of a piece, from the wood panels and marquetry to the sunburst glass, from the letters outside to the letters on the floor, from the Moderne flourishes to the Formica table tops and plain wooden chairs. The customers are a mix of locals, regulars, tourists and fans of classic cafés and post-war design. It has a warm atmosphere and a basic food menu, and is great for a fry-up breakfast, fish and chips and a pudding, or just a cup of tea or frothy coffee. Come for breakfast before moving on to Shoreditch and your day will be nicely set up. Outside is the Bethnal Green Road Market which has excellent fruit and veg stalls.

i OPEN MON-SAT 7-4, CLOSED SUN

▶ 332 BETHNAL GREEN ROAD TEL 020 7739 4873

WEST Swimming pool and Turkish baths Just behind the fantastically wonky church of St Luke's on Old Street is the recently and marvellously renovated Ironmonger Row Baths. Walk from Old Street station to St Luke's whose highly unusual obelisk spire, designed by Nicholas Hawksmoor, is a local landmark. The church (Grade I listed) dates from the 1730s and as it was built on marshy land, it suffered quickly from subsidence. Go to the back and you'll see the effects this has had on the building in the form of strangely distorted windows. No wonder it was eventually closed in 1964, and left to decay for forty years until it was rescued and taken over by the London Symphony Orchestra who now use it for concerts, rehearsals and recordings.

From the back of the church, it's just a short walk to the Ironmonger Row Baths across the way. These were built in 1931, and they inspired Nell Dunn's play *Steaming* (first produced in 1981) which is set in a steamy, Turkish baths threatened with closure. A few years later, Roger Deakin wrote an evocative account of his visit to Ironmonger Row in *Waterlog* (1996). The baths always have been at the heart of the community here – there are still laundry facilities – and it's wonderful to come to swim and sweat in somewhere so full of history and character. The main 30.5m pool is beautiful: calm, pale, light, with tall windows and a lovely, curved blue and white ceiling, and it still has the original tiered wooden seats for the crowds who came to watch the diving and the racing. Downstairs, the spa has all you need in the way of Turkish baths, steam rooms, showers and the large, original relaxation room. The spa has mixed, male, and female sessions and it is worth phoning in advance to check the busy times, and booking if necessary to ensure you get the day you want. A swim can be spontaneous though, and this is as lovely a place to do a few lengths as any in London.

i CHECK WEBSITE FOR OPENING TIMES AS THEY MAY VARY (GENERALLY MON-FRI 6.30AM-9.30PM, SAT 9-6, SUN 9-6)

❯❯ 1 NORMAN STREET   TEL 020 3642 5520

@ WWW.BETTER.ORG.UK

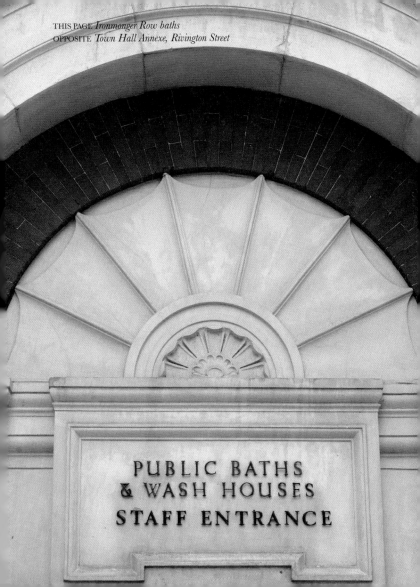

PUBLIC BATHS
& WASH HOUSES
STAFF ENTRANCE

MORE LIGHT MORE POWER

Where to stay

As befits a place that is as of the moment as Shoreditch, there are several stylish hotels whose aesthetics and atmospheres make them places to be and be seen.

Shoreditch House is part of the Soho House group and caters for both member and non-members. Its room rates vary quite wildly, and sometimes the prices drop dramatically. Check the calendar carefully as there no real pattern to the prices, although Sundays and mid-week days are often cheaper. Guests get fantastic facilities (spa, rooftop pool, table tennis tables, bars, reading room) and a superb location above Pizza East and close to everything in Spitalfields and Shoreditch.

⟩⟩ EBOR STREET TEL 020 7739 5040

@ WWW.SHOREDITCHHOUSE.COM

Ace Hotel The opening of the Ace Hotel in late 2013 signalled the fact that Shoreditch had well and truly reinvented itself and arrived. There are hip, cool Ace Hotels in places like Portland and Palm Springs and New York which act as magnets for style-hunters, and the Shoreditch outpost is now doing exactly the same. The hotel is, in fact, the old Crowne Plaza but with a new look grafted on. The structure remains the same, but the place has been transformed by a reconfiguration of pub-

OPPOSITE *Ace Hotel*

lic spaces into understatedly stylish areas, and by updating the rooms. This has been achieved by clever interior design, furniture which is a mix of vintage and specially commissioned, the light fittings which are industrial and modern, the use of subtle, natural materials (denim, cork, wood) and the mix of pale, dark and neutral colours which go so well with concrete. The spacious public areas are places to socialise, meet, drink, chat, read, listen to music, and work (I love the long, long table where everyone sits with their laptops and coffees). The bedrooms are still plain boxes but they have been cleverly fitted out with witty touches, macramé art, 'curated shelves', and interesting hotel stationery.

You don't have to be a hotel guest to enjoy the Ace. The lobby areas, photo booth, bar, café, flower shop and restaurant are all available to non-residents, as is the hotel's restaurant, Hoi Polloi. This is done out in what could be described as a smart Scandinavian school canteen look, and is a latter-day Festival of Britain interior. The menus are mad and very long – the restaurant is open all day for every conceivable meal and eating moment. The atmosphere is buzzy and Hoi Polloi is perfect for meeting friends, reading newspapers, taking afternoon tea, or simply recovering from a Shoreditch tour.

▶ ACE HOTEL 100 SHOREDITCH HIGH STREET TEL 020 7613 9800
   HOI POLLOI TEL 020 8880 6100
@ WWW.ACEHOTEL/LONDON

Airbnb allows you to rent a room, an apartment, or an entire home for a day, weekend, week, month, year direct from the owner. All budgets and tastes appear to be catered for in Shoreditch, and this is the modern way to find an affordable, flexible, self-catering base for a stay here.

@ WWW.AIRBNB.CO.UK

The Hoxton When you realise that the Hoxton was created by the same people who were behind Pret (who have since sold it) it all makes sense. All the rooms, apart from a small number of individually designed suites, are the same: compact, thoughtfully designed with no unnecessary stuff but with useful bits and pieces such as decent desks, breakfast bags, corkscrews, free wi-fi, coffee and fresh milk in fridges. The rates can be surprisingly fair for the location (Sunday is the cheapest night) and especially for a place with such good design values – the lobby looks like a sort of postmodern country lodge, complete with stag's head. Because of all this, it's very popular so it is worth booking ahead.

》 81 GREAT EASTERN STREET TEL 020 7550 1000
@ WWW.HOXTONHOTEL.COM

Acknowledgements

Thank you to Julie Crofts, Rachel Fenn and Chloe Evans for helping me sample cafés and shops.

Thank you to Nicola Beauman for sharing lunches and excellent recommendations.

Thank you to Amanda Carr and Jane Kellock of The Women's Room blog for the event at which I won the prize of a night in the Ace Hotel.

Thank you to Lydia Sage and Angela Burdett for their enthusiasm and support.

Thank you to Tom, Alice and Phoebe Brocket for sharing coffee, pizza, doughnuts, Brick Lane and photo booths.

Thank you to Simon Brocket for all the years of coming to London with me, and for the visits to Shoreditch for flowers, breakfasts, lunches, and bagels.

And finally, many, many thanks to Sarah Rock who created the beautiful design for this book.

Text and photographs copyright © Jane Brocket 2015

First published 2015 by Yarnstorm Press
www.yarnstormpress.co.uk

Set in Baskerville and Gotham
Design © Sarah Rock 2015

Printed by Lavenham Press, Suffolk
978-1-910233-04-7

TRAVEL
with a
BROCKET
in your
POCKET